FARSI CHILDREN'S BOOK

The Adventures of Tom Sawyer

WAI CHEUNG

©Copyright, 2017, by Wai Cheung and Maestro Publishing Group
All rights reserved.

No part of this book may be reproduced or transmitted in any form or by any means, electronic or mechanical, including photocopying, recording or by any information storage and retrieval system, without permission in writing of the copyright owner.

Printed in the United States of America.

ABOUT THE BOOK

Raise your children in a bilingual fashion with this bilingual coloring book that captures the magic of Tom Sawyer's story along with a dual language storytelling that is perfect for parents who want to raise their children in a bilingual environment.

CONTENTS

Plate 1 3

Plate 2 5

Plate 3 7

Plate 4 9

Plate 5 11

Plate 6 13

Plate 7 15

Plate 8 17

This page intentionally left blank.

تام ساير توانست بعضی از دوستانش را وادار کند نرده ها را برایش رنگ کنند، حتی با این که وظیفۀ خودش بود.

Plate 1

تام همچنین عاشق یکی نجیر شد، اما رابطهٔ آن‌ها مدت طولانی پایدار نبود

Plate 2

Tom and his best friend Huckleberry Finn saw it all at once; then Injun Joe actually murdered Dr. Robinson and let Muff Potter take the blame!

تام به همراه بهترین دوستش هاکلبری فین دککه را دیدند که اینجان جو دکتر رابینسون را به قتل رساند و اجازه داد ماف پاتر تقصیر را بر عهده بگیرد

Plate 3

Plate 4

Plate 5

Tom and Huck searched a haunted house for buried treasure and witnessed the escaped Injun Joe with a box that could only contain one thing.

تام و هاک در یک خانه متروکه به دنبال گنج بودند که فرار اینجان جو را به همراه یک جعبه که می تواند فقط شامل یک چیز باشد دیدند.

13

Plate 6

تام متوجه شد که انجیل جو طلاها را در یک غار که زیاد هم از شهر دور نیست، نگهداری می‌کند.

Plate 7

Tom and Huck went back to the cave to retrieve the gold, and Tom convinced Huck to allow the Widow Douglas to adopt him as her own.

تام و هاک به غار رفتند تا طلاها را بردارند و تام، هاک را متقاعد کرد که به بیوه داگلاس اجازه دهد که او را به فرزندی بپذیرد.

Plate 8

This page intentionally left blank.

ABOUT THE BOOK

Raise your children in a bilingual fashion with this bilingual coloring book that captures the magic of Tom Sawyer's story along with a dual language storytelling that is perfect for parents who want to raise their children in a bilingual environment.

Printed in the USA
CPSIA information can be obtained
at www.ICGtesting.com
LVHW080047160324
774593LV00006B/872